A Rule of Life

for Daily Christian Living

by
Fr Michael Woodgate

*All booklets are published thanks to the
generous support of the members of the
Catholic Truth Society*

CATHOLIC TRUTH SOCIETY
PUBLISHERS TO THE HOLY SEE

Contents

Reasons for a Rule of Life 3
    Everyday living 3
    Value of a Rule of Life 3
    Domestic Church 5
    Preparing to make our Rule 6

Elements of a Rule of Life 9
    Mass 9
    Prayer 10
    Where to start in prayer 13
    Devotions 14
    Confession or Reconciliation 15
    Fasting, self-denial and abstinence 17
    Bible reading, spiritual reading and study . 19
    Almsgiving 22
    Retreats, days of recollection 24
    Service 26
    Spiritual direction 28
    Make a beginning 29

Reasons for a Rule of Life

Everyday living

"Holiness is not an optional extra to the process of creation, but rather the whole point of it." This quotation comes from Donald Nicholl in a remarkable book entitled "Holiness", published in 1981. "Rule of Life" is an expression we don't often hear nowadays and even religious congregations tend not to use it though, of course, they still live their lives according to a rule. Some readers may remember that television series called "Bless me, Father" in which the Mother Superior's favourite saying would be: "But it's our Rule, Father", spoken to the parish priest to reject any suggestion he might make. But a Rule of Life (or whatever we want to call it) can be an enormous help to ordinary Catholics and Christians who really do want to follow Christ. In recent years the Rule of St Benedict (which is still a basis for many religious orders) has been re-interpreted for lay Christians by a number of different writers.

Value of a Rule of Life

When we think of holiness, we tend to think of saints and immediately dissociate ourselves from it and them, admiring both from a distance. But if we have been baptized, we are already "saints-in-the-making", as someone has called us and St Paul addresses all Christians as saints. So how do we become holy, how do we encourage our Christian life to grow and mature into holiness? Yes, by prayer, by taking our part in the Mass, by receiving Holy Communion, by good works and so on. The list is easy to make, not so easy to practise. Our wills are often weak; we allow so many other things to get in the way and take priority. This is where a personal Rule of Life can be invaluable. "But surely," you may say, "we don't want to reduce our living faith, our love for God, our discipleship of Christ, to a list of rules?" No, of course not; but remember that the word "rule" really means "regular" and so a Rule of Life is something to help us live our lives in regular contact with God, welcoming each new day, week, month or Church's season as a new opportunity to love and serve Our Lord and our fellow men and women. Because of human frailty we need reminders, we need practical help, we need guidance in doing this. Above all, we need to acquire good habits to live out the Christian life. It was St Bernard who said, "Take care of order and order will take care of you". The word "disciple" and the word "discipline" both come from the same Latin word meaning "to learn". So our personal discipline helps and encourages our discipleship.

Domestic Church

A Rule of Life is usually regarded as a very personal aid to Christian living, but there is no reason why it should not be drawn up for a married couple or even a whole family. After all, we are used to "Family Fast Days", and monastic rules (cf the Rule of St Benedict) are always for a religious family. A family rule needs the consultation of all the members of the family if old enough to contribute. Primary (and possibly even a little older) school-aged children will probably enjoy feeling part of such decision-making. Individual members of the family may want to make some personal resolutions of their own, of course. It may prove a means of bringing married couples closer to one another and indeed whole families. To know that others in the family are all making that special effort can give real support to each individual. After all, every family, every household is what is sometimes called "the domestic Church". It is always a joy when one sees a whole family come not only to Mass, but also to the sacrament of reconciliation and some of us are old enough to remember the slogan made popular many years ago by Fr Peyton and his rosary crusade: "The family that prays together stays together". A family or married couple's Rule of Life can help to do the same thing.

What we must not do is to allow our Rule to become our master. It should always be a good servant, never ruling our lives and never becoming an end in itself. The "end" or purpose is our loving service of God and neighbour and therefore we must always allow room for the Holy Spirit to be our ultimate guide, our ultimate leader on the pilgrim way to holiness and so to heaven. As we know from the Gospels, Our Lord had harsh words for those who put rules before their love for God and their fellows.

Having said that, perhaps we could think of our Rule as a good companion, adaptable when necessary, helpful at all times, and ready to keep us going when we tend to flag. When we draw it up, we need to avoid fussiness, overmuch detail, anything impractical or complicated. The Church herself of course, has given us some very basic rules for our Christian lives such as: Mass on all Sundays and Holydays of Obligation, the need to make a sacramental confession and receive Holy Communion at least once a year; abstinence of some kind on a Friday, fasting on Ash Wednesday and Good Friday. These, however, are minimal and if we did nothing more, our love for Our Lord would seem rather cold and almost formal.

Preparing to make our Rule

Before making a Rule of Life we need to pray for the guidance of the Holy Spirit and for His wisdom. It should never be so demanding that we often fail to keep it, nor so undemanding that it is hardly worth having. We could take our guide from St Benedict who advocates moderation so far as his monks are concerned. Some other religious orders would have much tougher Rules. It is true that some lay Christians are called to make what seem heroic efforts in their daily living out of the Christian life and all of us might be called to these from time to time, but for the great majority this is not so. So what should we include? One thing we need to watch is our use of time, so we need to keep that in mind and guard against the wasting of time in our daily lives.

We often hear that expression "quality time" these days, and a good parent knows how he or she must make quality time for their children. Each spouse (whether parents or not) must do the same for the other. Likewise with our friends - we need to ensure that we make time for them and not always expect them to make the time for us. Relationships and friendships are not intended to be static. Indeed, they cannot be, for they will either grow or deteriorate depending upon how each party manages them. Our relationship with God is - or should be - a very close one and therefore we need to set aside quality time for Him every day as well as make special times during the week, month or year. This is what we are setting out in our Rule of Life, well aware of how our relationship with Him can either grow or deteriorate.

Inevitably, there is something very personal about a Rule of Life and it could give the impression that it is all about "me and my God" with concern for neighbour thrown in as an afterthought. If this is how it seems, then let us remind ourselves that we are members of the Body of Christ and if one member suffers then all the other members suffer with it, as St Paul puts it. It is also true that if one member is weak through lack of perseverance, then all the other members are weakened. By trying to give God our very best and doing so in a disciplined and loving way, we are strengthening the whole Body, as our fellow-Christians, we trust, are doing the same thing.

It should go without saying that the Rule of the single person living alone is going to be somewhat different from that of those who live as members of a household. Indeed, some parts of a Rule can be undertaken by a family together. One still sees families, if not so common as at one time, coming to confession at regular intervals and many undertake a family practice on Fridays - some shared act of self-denial or even fasting. Of course, a Rule of Life is personal but it helps greatly when we know others are keeping or trying to keep theirs too. One reason why we usually manage to do something special or extra during Lent is because we know we are not alone. Christians all over the world are trying to do something special too and that is both encouraging and supportive, as we were suggesting in the previous paragraph. Here, then, are some suggestions with comments which might help in drawing up our personal Rule of Life.

Elements of a Rule of Life

Mass

All Catholics are expected to join in the celebration of Mass every Sunday of the year and every Holyday of Obligation unless prevented by sickness, infirmity or some urgent duty. It should, of course, be our joy and delight to join with fellow Catholics in offering the Holy Sacrifice of Christ to His Father, and receiving the wonderful gift of Himself. Somebody once said that when it comes to the Eucharist (and this is equally true of our prayer generally) absence makes the heart grow colder. Our Blessed Lord said "Do this..." and if we don't, then surely our love for Him is waning. If we allow tiredness or bad weather or a late night or even that voice that comes straight from the Evil One saying "You're not worthy, after doing so and so..." It's amazing how clever the Evil One is at finding us excuses which sound so reasonable and even pious!

It is good to attend Mass also on weekdays and so in working out our Rule, we should see how and when this is possible. We might in particular attend on such days as Ash Wednesday, our parish's feast of title, the anniversaries of loved ones and All Souls' Day,

Solemnities and the more important feast days. Unlike Sunday Mass, which can often be a busy and even noisy or distracted time for the best of reasons, an ordinary weekday Mass usually offers an opportunity for a more prayerful celebration.

Why not aim for a mid-week Mass, or perhaps one on Friday which, as we are reminded later, has a special character, being the day when we remember Christ's sacrificial death for us? Some parishes find their Saturday morning Mass well-attended because it is for many a non-working day.

If we are sick, especially if for more than a week, we should ensure that our parish priest knows so that we can be brought the Blessed Sacrament at home or in hospital. When we go on holiday, we need to seek out the Sunday and Holy Day Mass times as soon as possible.

Prayer

You do not have to read far into the Gospels to discover that Jesus was a man of prayer; it was an essential part of his daily life. He would rise early in the morning and go to a place where he could be as solitary as possible, perhaps into the hills behind the Lake of Galilee.

We have a few precious glimpses of Jesus at prayer, when he would open his heart to the Father and converse with him. The most poignant of these occasions, of course, is that time on Holy Thursday in the Garden of

Gethsemane when his prayer was so intense that sweat poured down his face like drops of blood. St John in his wonderful chapter seventeen lets us hear Our Lord's high priestly prayer (as it is called) when, amongst other things, he prayed for his apostles. Earlier on, it was as a result of seeing their Master at prayer that the apostles asked him to teach them to pray and so he taught them the *Our Father*. So it goes without saying that prayer will have a key place in our Rule of Life.

'Absence makes the heart grow...colder?' With regard to our prayer, yes it does! The less we pray, the less we want to pray and so our love for God cools. This is why regular, daily prayer is so important. We need to decide when and how long to pray each day. We need to decide what we are going to do during that time of prayer. For some, may be for many people, the traditional practice of praying soon after they get up in the morning and then just before they go to bed still works; for others lunch time is a good opportunity, especially if they work near a church that is open at that time (as in many of our bigger towns and cities) or if they are at home and the rest of the family is out. Some, whether at home or in the office, visit one of the internet sites which display a theme for prayer that day.

It is also good practice to spend a longer time of prayer each week at least, perhaps with a passage of Scripture, e.g. the Sunday readings. This may also be a good way of preparing for Holy Communion. What we do in prayer will vary from person to person. Some may want to combine meditation and intercession by using the rosary, not necessarily confining oneself to the (now) four traditional mysteries. Others may want to take just a verse or a word from Scripture and repeat it in a contemplative way, perhaps letting it lead to a time of silence. One very useful practice is to review the past day (or 24 hours) and see where and how we have responded to God; to notice what He has been saying to us through others and in all kinds of ways. A growing number of Christians find it helpful to say one or more of the Offices from the official Prayer of the Church or an adaptation of one of these. CTS publish a number of very helpful little books about prayer and different ways of prayer, including one with an Office. You may also want to ask help from your priest or a religious, or someone you know who is experienced in leading a prayerful life, and there is bound to be such a person in your own parish. Prayer needs to be balanced, which is why the older books used to advocate a structure of prayer based on the mnemonic ACTS - Adoration, Contrition, Thanksgiving and Supplication.

Of course, our prayer should grow and change as our relationship with God deepens and this is where having someone to whom we can turn for advice or encouragement can be very valuable. There will be times in our lives when prayer becomes (as we would put it) difficult, dry or even boring. These are often the times when our relationship with God is deepening and so we need to change our way of prayer. On the other hand, it could indicate exactly the opposite. Again, a guide or spiritual director can help.

Intercession is an important part of prayer and is greatly needed by the Church and the world. Some people have a scheme for this; others may simply take the daily paper or radio and TV news and pick out items for prayer. This can also be a challenging part of our prayer, because we should never pray for someone or something without being prepared to do something about it, should God ask us.

Where to start in prayer

For those who are new to prayer, perhaps having just been received into the Church, it is best to begin with a simple, structured approach. You may well have been given a prayer book such as *A Simple Prayer Book* (published by CTS) and there you will find prayers for morning and evening. Using these, and certainly the structure of these, will help ground you in the habit of prayer. But don't recite them like a parrot! Say them slowly and thoughtfully - a little done well is better than rushing through. Always give yourself time to settle into prayer, being aware of your body, your feelings, any little aches and pains, and any noises you can hear and then gradually let them go. Always begin with the sign of the cross - the greatest Christian symbol. Find a time at least each week, (better each day) in which to pray the rosary and there are plenty of little books to help you (e.g. *Praying the Rosary with the Saints* and *A Simple Rosary Book* both from CTS). Gradually, you will develop your own style of prayer, and discover what helps most. A great teacher of prayer, the Benedictine monk Dom John Chapman, once said: "Pray as you best can pray and not as you can't".

Devotions

The Catholic Church has a rich store of devotional practices, some of which may well be incorporated into a Rule of Life. The most obvious, perhaps, because it springs directly from the Mass, is Adoration of the Blessed Sacrament and Benediction. Many parishes provide an opportunity for this each week, but if you cannot be present for whatever reason Our Blessed Lord is always present in the tabernacle and we can adore him and pray to him there. It is sometimes simply called "A Visit to the Blessed Sacrament" and so we might make a commitment to visit at least once a week, making sure that the church will be open.

Almost every Catholic church has, around its walls, the Stations of the Cross and many Catholics make a point of following Our Lord in his journey to the Cross during

Lent, but you might like to do this at other times as well, perhaps as a Friday devotion.

A film which made quite an impact recently is *Into the Great Silence* which comes from the great Carthusian mother house "La Grande Chartreuse" in France. One of the features of the monks' life is to pray as a community in church in the middle of the night. You may be one of those people who tend to wake during the night and find it difficult to get to sleep again. Rather than tossing and turning, why not have a period of prayer? It could be the rosary, a litany (someone once composed a special night litany for such occasions), or a short office and there are one or two in existence, or you could use all or part of the Office of Readings in the Divine Office. If you fall asleep before completing your prayer, so much the better! Of course, you may be a good sleeper, but actually want to get up for some nocturnal prayer as a special offering to God.

Confession or Reconciliation

The Church expects us to make our confession at least during the period of Eastertide (Ash Wednesday to Trinity Sunday), but any Catholic who really loves God will want to do this more often. Of course, we must always celebrate the sacrament if we have done something seriously wrong, but every sin spoils our friendship with the Lord and the grace we receive from the sacrament strengthens our resolve and our ability to love and serve Him better, provided we are truly penitent and take some steps to do this. There are many benefits from celebrating the sacrament of reconciliation and you will appreciate these more and more as you avail yourself of it. One is that it helps to develop and sharpen the conscience. It has been said of some of the saints that they were the greatest sinners, meaning that the more they looked into the face of Christ, the more they realized how and where they failed to reflect his likeness. Regular and reasonably frequent confession makes us more accountable to God for our actions and also makes us more ready and willing to forgive others, as we realize only too well our own failings and the rich mercy of God's love.

Some Catholics make their confession every month (or even more frequently), some at least four times a year (e.g. before Christmas, Easter, during the summer perhaps at Assumption-tide, and then again in the autumn, perhaps in October), others only before Christmas and Easter. You will have to decide what you are going to do, maybe beginning with three or four times a year and then increasing the frequency as your love for God grows.

For many Catholics, their visit to the confessional is also when they seek and receive spiritual direction, though this is not always the best time when there is a queue waiting. It is always best, if you think your visit may hold things up, to wait until last or to go at a time when there are not usually many penitents. You can, of course, make an appointment with the priest, especially if you explain that you need some specific direction or advice which could take a little time. After all, the sacrament of reconciliation is one of the priest's most important (and rewarding) ministries, though we need to be sure that we are reasonable in our request for his time.

Fasting, self-denial and abstinence

Our Lord asks all of us, each in his or her own way, to do penance. Some of this is given to us by the Church, e.g. we should abstain from meat or some other food (or alcoholic drink, or some form of amusement, or devote time to extra prayer or some good work for another, etc) on all Fridays (unless it happens to be a Solemnity). This helps to remind us of our Lord's great sacrifice for us and acts as something very small that we can offer to Him. Ash Wednesday and Good Friday are days of both abstinence and fasting. Fasting means having one main meal only and two collations (what we might call "snacks" or light refreshment), but we might want to eat even less than that.

In addition, we should make some kind of act of self-denial during Lent and also observe the Family Fast Days recommended by our Bishops in October and Lent. We might also want to keep a fast day just before Christmas, maybe on 23rd December. We need to be clear about the need to do penance or, to use a more inclusive word, to mortify ourselves. Quite simply, it is a way of saying "no" to ourselves. We know how weak our wills can be and how easy it is to give into our bodies. The problem of so-called "binge-drinking" and much (though not all) excess bodily weight so prevalent in our own society is due to an inability to deny oneself and, of course, having the means to do it. The need to slim or go on a diet has nothing to do with Christian teaching about fasting and mortification. These are undertaken to strengthen us to do God's will, to make reparation for sin, and to give glory to God. There will be those who say that fasting and self-denial are fine if you want to raise money for charity, but as a spiritual exercise they, along with other forms of mortification, are things of the past and a rather unhealthy aspect of Catholicism. They may also tell you that these things are against nature. But as Fr Louis Bouyer says in one of his books, the life which by-passes penance is no more natural than the life which embraces it. No, he says, it is not against nature, but it is supernatural. He then goes on to point out how it is a sharing (albeit tiny) in the Cross of Christ and to understand the meaning of the Cross it is not sufficient to look at it but to stretch oneself upon it.

Self-denial - in its various forms - also reminds us that we are engaged in spiritual warfare. The Devil is out to separate us from God and the ancient fathers and mothers of the Church were very aware of this. Yes, we are already, through our baptism, the sons and daughters of God and have nothing to fear from the powers of evil, provided that we are faithful to God and fully armed against those powers. Self-denial strengthens our will to say "no" to temptation, to say "no" to ourselves when self wants the upper hand. One of the aspects of Lent is that of re-arming ourselves for spiritual warfare, however politically incorrect such language may sound today. The ultimate self-denial for our Blessed Lord was the Cross and we are called to share in his victory, at the same time sharing in his battle, as we were indicating a little earlier. One of the most powerful stories in Scripture, though rather tucked away, is when King David asks for water to quench his thirst, but because it has put his men at risk from attack to bring it to him, he pours it out on the ground. What a waste? What an act of self-denial! What a sacrifice!

Bible reading, spiritual reading and study

Since our faith and our knowledge of the Catholic faith needs to go on growing it is good to form a habit of regular study and reading. There are some good Catholic Bible commentaries which will help us understand the Scriptures more intelligently and some parishes run Bible study groups. Many people are helped by publications such as *Scripture in Church* or *Magnificat*, which have devotional commentaries for both Sunday and weekday Mass readings.

An ancient way of reading the Bible which has been much revived in recent years is what is known as *Lectio Divina,* literally meaning "Spiritual Reading", but it is spiritual reading of a very focused and special kind whose emphasis is on prayerful reflection rather than study. Take a passage of Scripture (maybe one of the readings for Sunday or weekday Mass) and read it through very slowly. Read it again and even again. Then, at the last reading stop wherever a word or phrase attracts your attention. Repeat it, savour it, and allow the mind to roam around it. Pray about it or with it. Then be silent as you continue to contemplate it - or rather God. Blessed Columba Marmion, a Benedictine monk, put it like this: "We read, under the eye of God, until the heart is touched and leaps into flame." Indeed, *Lectio Divina* is a splendid way of letting the Holy Spirit lead you into deeper prayer.

We would do well to read also *The Catechism of the Catholic Church*, concentrating on one section at a time. There are also abbreviated versions available now. Our faith can often be enthused and strengthened by reading the life of a saint or some great Christian man or woman and your parish may have a library or a good repository. CTS has a large range of booklets on the lives of the saints at modest prices, and other Catholic bookshops can also advise you on Scripture commentaries of all kinds. It might be helpful to work out a reading plan, perhaps on a monthly basis and again, remember your priest or someone whose wisdom and judgement you can trust could help you here.

Other books can be read as *Lectio Divina*, e.g. *The Imitation of Christ* by Thomas a Kempis, *The Practice of the Presence of God* by Brother Lawrence or *The Cloud of Unknowing* by an unknown English, medieval writer; or *Prayer* by Urs von Balthasar, a 20 century Jesuit, and *Revelations of Divine Love* by Julian of Norwich. But choose carefully - there are many excellent writers on prayer and the spiritual life but you may not be ready for them yet.

There is plenty of good literature which would certainly not be labeled "spiritual" but can nourish and enrich the spirit. Some would be novels, biographies, autobiographies, others poetry, even plays. Films and theatre, carefully and sensibly chosen, can do the same. Some would have a distinctively Christian or Catholic basis; others may be more challenging and so help us to think more deeply about our faith. Your parish may have a library, perhaps even a reading circle and there is always the public library.

So far, we have not mentioned music and yet this has played such a leading role in the Church's liturgy throughout the ages. But besides all that has been written specifically for the Church (and plainchant is the most enduring example), there is much, usually labelled "secular", that can lift our spirits to great heights and relax us at the same time. Hymns and religious songs, old or new, may find a place in your actual time of prayer. Such music as the chants of Taizé and those of Margaret Rizza, are a feature of much contemporary corporate worship, but may be used for personal devotion. If you enjoy singing but you suspect others don't appreciate your talent, then why not let rip where no one can hear you? Some hymns, incidentally, sung or not, make fine prayers and can teach some good theology at the same time. The eucharistic hymns of St Thomas Aquinas, for example, can inspire one's love for the Mass and the Blessed Sacrament.

Almsgiving

Remember the Gospel story of the widow's mite and be generous in what you give to God and the work and upkeep of His Church. We should work out carefully how much we can give both to the parish (and second collection) and to charitable causes each week and be as generous as possible. We may well do this on a percentage basis, first deducting what we pay in income tax, council tax and national insurance (i.e. what we owe to the State and civic authorities for services provided). Some Christians (often non-Catholics), actually give what is called a tithe, i.e. a tenth of their income. Could we afford something approaching that or perhaps a twentieth? For the Jewish people of Jesus' time, the tithe was what you owed the synagogue, but your charitable giving did not begin until after you had paid this. It is most important to ensure regular and generous giving and it almost beggars belief to see someone put a pound coin or less into the collection bag on a Sunday and then think nothing of opening a bottle of wine costing at least three times as much, for their lunch! Almsgiving is a timely reminder that all we have comes from God and therefore even our money is not our own - we have it on trust from God and must account to him for it. And don't think, when deciding how much to give, in terms of your earned income. What about your investments, however small? They are adding to your income (unless the Stock Market crashes!), and so you should take them into account too, even the modest sum you have with the Post Office. Our almsgiving should also remind us of God's great generosity, not least His self-giving upon the Cross as the price paid for our redemption.

Of course, there will be times when, in addition to our regular giving, we shall be challenged to give more sacrificially - a national or international disaster, a charity in desperate need of new funds and so on. So far as charitable giving in general is concerned, a priest once said that he tended to concentrate his personal giving on Church or Christian-based charities as the more secular-based ones could look for their money from non-Christian or nominal-Christian sources. For example, charities supporting pro-life activities or mission or those persecuted for their Christian faith have to rely on Christian giving for the bulk of their finances. However, we all have our favourite charities and we can only support a limited number, otherwise our giving will be so diffuse that it will help no one very much.

Retreats, days of recollection

It is good, if we possibly can, to make an annual retreat - either a week-end or from Monday-Friday or even longer. Many of us may have to be content with a day or perhaps several separate days a year. A retreat is not the same as a pilgrimage or a conference. It is a time for specifically deepening our prayer life and relationship with God and for this we need some silence and some solitude. Some parishes organize retreats or days of recollection/reflection and if we are an Extraordinary Minister of Holy Communion, then we have already promised to make such a day on an annual basis. Such times help us to renew and re-energize our spiritual lives, to reflect on what's been happening in our lives and generally help us to move forward. Increasingly, parishes or deaneries or even Churches Together are organizing Weeks of Guided Prayer, as they are called. These are retreats in daily life with the participants meeting up with a prayer guide each day for a week or so, who will give them a passage or two of Scripture for their prayerful reflection. They are invited to share with their guide what has happened during their prayer and he or she will listen, encourage, challenge and suggest as needed. Some will be familiar with this kind of retreat in a residential setting, often known as individually-guided, and which can provide enormous help to so many who want to take their prayer more seriously, but who often lead very busy lives. It should go without saying that the prayer guides will have received training for their work through one of the growing number of courses across the country.

This is just one of the many different kinds of retreat available these days which try to cater for different needs at different times. It is worth buying a copy of the annual journal published by the National Retreat Association simply entitled *Retreats* and which will give you a list county by county, of the retreats arranged for the current year. As the list is ecumenical, you will need to check exactly what is available by way of the sacraments, e.g., not all retreats would include a Catholic Mass. It might be a good idea to check out what you have chosen with your parish priest or someone in the parish who is knowledgeable about these things. However, be assured that *Retreats* is a Christian publication and does not include so-called New Age programmes. Why not suggest to your parish priest that there be a parish residential retreat or a week of guided prayer? But be warned - he may ask you to organize it! And why not? The National Retreat Association can always help.

Service

We should all be involved in some way in the life of our parish and be able to offer some regular service. Many of us may be doing this already, e.g. as Extraordinary Ministers, Readers, Servers, Musicians, Catechists, Flower Arrangers, Welcomers, Parish Council members, Cleaners, Administrative assistants in the parish office, assisting or even running the Repository, visiting the sick, the elderly, the bereaved, helping with mother and toddler groups, youth groups, those with special needs, lunch clubs, or be involved with prayer groups, marriage preparation, Pro-life, Justice and Peace, local Churches Together, hospital chaplaincy visiting, etc.

Charity, we are told, begins at home, so maybe we need to start there. Within your family or household, do you assist with domestic chores, with shopping, with the garden, with the pets, with visitors, with correspondence, telephone calls, emails etc? Or do you tend to leave it all to one person? Do you make too many demands upon one member of the family? This is already beginning to sound like a list for self-examination, and it could go on! Perhaps a neighbour needs a helping hand - someone who struggles to hang up their washing because of age or infirmity or excessive pressure on their life at the moment. A blind neighbour may appreciate having a reader. Your child's school, too, may need more volunteer help in many different ways, so what are your skills and gifts? Maybe you belong to a society or organization in which you have always expected someone else to be the secretary, treasurer, lift-giver, committee member, coffee-maker - could this be the time for you to offer your services? If you are married (with or without a family), how much quality time do you spend together? How often do you go out for a meal, or to the cinema or theatre, a quiz night, a drink in the local, an exhibition, or have an away-day to some place of interest, or where you can simply relax and enjoy one another's company?

But there are also the many other ways of assisting the wider community outside the parish through all kinds of voluntary work and your local library should be able to put you in touch with some of these.

A word of warning - don't try and do too much and go for the things where your gifts or charisms can be used! The problem with many parishes is that too few people are doing too much and too many are doing very little. Sometimes this is because they are not encouraged, or even feel that they are not wanted because everything appears to be going along very nicely! Have a look at the Beatitudes (St Matthew 5:1-11) and see how Our Lord sets out a list of the Church's needs. In your parish, e.g., how is mercy being shown to the needy (the homeless, the addicted, the mentally ill etc), how are issues of justice and peace (righteousness) being catered for, what concern is there for the persecuted, how are people being helped to see God more clearly through emphasis on prayer and spiritual growth, what care is there for the bereaved? The list could go on. God doesn't ask every one of us to do all these things, but He surely asks all of us to do something. The housebound might undertake intercession for particular causes, or write letters on behalf of prisoners of conscience, or correspond with those in prison who often have few, if any, who bother about them.

Spiritual direction

As you begin to take the Christian life more seriously (and, we trust, joyfully), you may well feel the need for what is called a spiritual director. It sounds a bit frightening perhaps, but this is someone with whom we can meet up on a regular basis (maybe once a month or less frequently) and with whom we can share what has been going on for us. At the root of it all will be our prayer, for that is both the wellspring and the springboard of all we do for God. It is also the place where we take all that we have been doing. But it is also the place where our spiritual lives need to go on growing and so affect all that we do. A spiritual director will ask us about our prayer, but not concentrate exclusively on it, for the whole of our life should be focused on God; if there are places where it isn't, a spiritual director may be able to help us to re-focus accordingly. Again, the National Retreat Association should be able to help you find a director or guide (if you prefer that more friendly sounding word). We will all have received direction or guidance through the sacrament of reconciliation, but the priest in the confessional rarely has time to give us all that we need in that respect. Not all priests or religious have this particular charism of spiritual direction, though increasingly priests are receiving specific training in the basics of it. However, across the country there is a large number of lay people, men and women, who have received some expert training, often after they have discovered that people approach them for help in their Christian lives - not so much in a formal way, but through the odd encounter, maybe after Mass or a parish meeting of some kind. There may well be one living near you! Finally...

Make a beginning

All that you have read so far may seem daunting and even off-putting, but remember that you are probably doing many of these things already and in any case they are guidelines, not hard and fast instructions. Their merit is that they have been tried and they emanate from a long tradition of Catholic faith and practice in which we are privileged to share.

Write out your Rule, sign and date it and be sure to review it from time to time, at least once a year. Circumstances change in all kinds of ways. Ask God to help you keep it generously.

Remember it is not a sin to break your Rule (unless it is a rule of the Church) and there are times when it is right to break it. What God asks for is our love and so a well-kept Rule means not just one where we can tick what we have done, but one where we are keeping it in the right spirit.

A Simple Prayer Book

Contains:
- Morning and Evening Prayer
- The Order of Mass
- The Rosary
- The Angelus
- Going to Confession
- Adoration and Benediction
- Prayers for various ocassions
- A summary of Church teaching and more

ISBN: 978 1 86082 259 9

CTS Code: D 665

Informative Catholic Reading

We hope that you have enjoyed reading this booklet.

If you would like to find out more about CTS booklets - we'll send you our free information pack and catalogue.

Please send us your details:

    Name ....

    Address ....

    ....

    ....

    Postcode ....

    Telephone ....

    Email ....

Send to: CTS, 40-46 Harleyford Road,
              Vauxhall, London
              SE11 5AY

Tel: 020 7640 0042
Fax: 020 7640 0046
Email: info@cts-online.org.uk